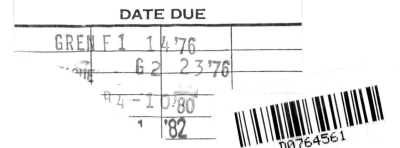

The Story of
MONTICELLO

By Norman Richards

Illustrations by Chuck Mitchell

CHILDRENS PRESS, CHICAGO

Sandy-haired Thomas Jefferson was fourteen years old in 1757 when he inherited a little mountain. It was called *Monticello*, which is "little mountain" in Italian. This was nineteen years before the American colonies declared their independence from England. So this mountain and the rest of the plantation were in the British colony of Virginia.

Many years earlier, when the Virginia colonists were beginning to make money from tobacco and building fine homes along the James River, Thomas Jefferson's father had taken an enormous claim on the frontier. It was a hundred miles northwest of Williamsburg in the Blue Ridge foothills. Thomas grew up here in what had once been the hunting grounds of the Tuscarora Indians.

Young Thomas liked nothing better than to roam the woods of the little mountain across the river from his home, and to hunt and fish there with his friends. He would climb to the top of this mountain where he could see for miles in all directions. Someday, he thought, he would build a house of his own upon this spot.

The boy, Thomas, was not always free to ride mountain trails and to explore. He had to go to school, first to Parson Douglas and then to Parson Maury. He learned Greek, Latin, and French among other things. His interests were as wide as the frontier country in which he was growing up. And his curious mind led him to read everything he could find.

When Thomas was seventeen, he went to William and Mary College in Williamsburg. It was a gay city with fine houses and stores. Sailing ships brought silks from China and fine furniture from England. Many ladies and gentlemen rode in their carriages, dressed in elegant clothes tailored in London and Paris.

Young Thomas entered into the gay life of the town. Sometimes he saw his distant cousin, Colonel George Washington, who was commander in chief of the Virginia troops, charged with defending the frontier from attacks by the French and Indians. He talked politics with Patrick Henry. He danced at the governor's palace. Sometimes he played his violin with a group there. He read law with George Wythe. He listened to arguments in the House of Burgesses.

Jefferson thought about the house he wanted to build, and since there were no architects in the colony, he studied architecture. He was charmed by the classic beauty of early Greek and Roman buildings. He looked at the homes of his wealthy friends who lived along the James River. Many of these houses were square, frame buildings with many outbuildings around them. A weaving house, a smokehouse, an icehouse, a laundry, a kitchen, and many others.

Thomas Jefferson was a most unusual young man. Many wealthy people of Williamsburg gave little thought to the poor farmers. But Jefferson believed that it was character and skill, not wealth, that set a man apart. He liked the honest, independent spirit of the farmers and often rode through the country between Williamsburg and his home helping these people with their legal problems. These stalwart men who had built their homes with their own hands and

cleared the land to make fields for their crops felt strongly about their rights as Americans.

A royal governor was in residence in the palace at Williamsburg, but King George III had paid little attention to his Virginia colony, and the laws were made by the Virginia men elected to the House of Burgesses.

Then, in 1765, the king needed money. He levied the first direct tax on Americans. It was called the Stamp Act. Many of the colonists were furious. They felt that they should not be taxed because they were not represented in England where the law was made. Heated arguments broke out in the House of Burgesses.

One day Thomas Jefferson stood in the doorway to the hall and listened to Patrick Henry give a dramatic speech asking that a strong protest be sent to the king. He attacked the king's government for taxing the colonies. One member shouted, "This is treason!" And Henry replied, "If this be treason, then make the most of it!"

The Stamp Act was finally repealed. But other British laws were passed to tax the colonists. There were troubled times and divided loyalties.

Thomas Jefferson agreed with Patrick Henry and the other patriots, and he loved the excitement of Williamsburg. Even so, he liked to get away to the

quiet of his mountain whenever he could. He decided to start building his house.

The plans he had drawn were for a thirty-five room mansion, although he knew it would take him many years to complete it. He also knew that his plans would be changed often as the house grew.

Before he could start to build, the top of the mountain had to be leveled off. Jefferson hired a contractor to do this work. He agreed to pay him 180 bushels of wheat and 24 bushels of corn from his plantation. Jefferson was rich in land, but often he had very little cash.

Jefferson's house would be different in many ways from the tidewater mansions of his friends. For one thing, it would be built on a mountain instead of by a river. Both east and west entrances would have stately white columns as so many of the ancient Greek and Roman buildings had. The house would have three stories, although it would look as though it had one. An eight-sided dome would rise over the center of the building. Windows would be placed so that the view from each was like a picture.

Jefferson did not like the look of the cluster of outbuildings around most plantation houses. He wanted to make these service buildings as much a part of the house as possible. He designed two long terraces that ended in small houses. The kitchen, cook's room,

smokehouse, servants' quarters, and the dairy would be put under the south terrace. Carriage house, icehouse, stables, and laundry would be under the north terrace. Covered passageways connecting the terraces and the house made it possible to get to any one of the service houses under cover in any kind of weather.

Almost as soon as the ground was leveled, Jefferson sent to England for window glass and hardware. All else needed for the house would come off the mountain. Bricks would be made from the clay there. Nails would be made in a little nail factory. Lumber would be cut from the woods.

Thomas Jefferson was elected to the House of

Burgesses, and so he spent many days traveling back and forth to Williamsburg.

The house grew slowly. The little house at the end of the south terrace was the first thing completed. It was to this house that Jefferson brought his bride one night in a blizzard. The carriage could not get through, so they finished the trip on horseback. Ever since, the little house has been known as Honeymoon Cottage.

People of Virginia talked about Jefferson's wonderful house that he called *Monticello*, after the mountain on which it was built. They were amazed to see the results of his inventive mind as the house grew.

Swivel chair

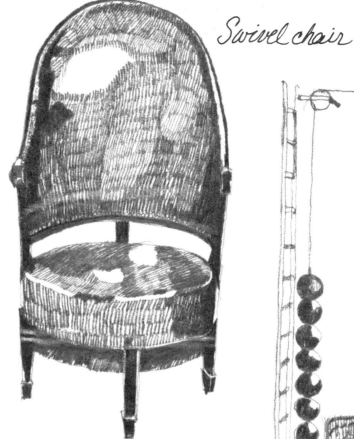

He built in revolving doors with shelves on one side. He put a weathervane on the roof. The unusual thing about it was that he had a pointer put inside the house so that he could tell wind direction without going outside. He designed a clock for the hall which had one face outside. It also told the day of the week. He designed a folding ladder that was used to wind the clock.

Tiny dumbwaiters concealed in the side of a fireplace carried food and dishes up and down, to and from, the dining room.

Mr. Jefferson designed much of the unusual furniture for the house, and even the draperies.

Fireplace
with
dumbwaiter

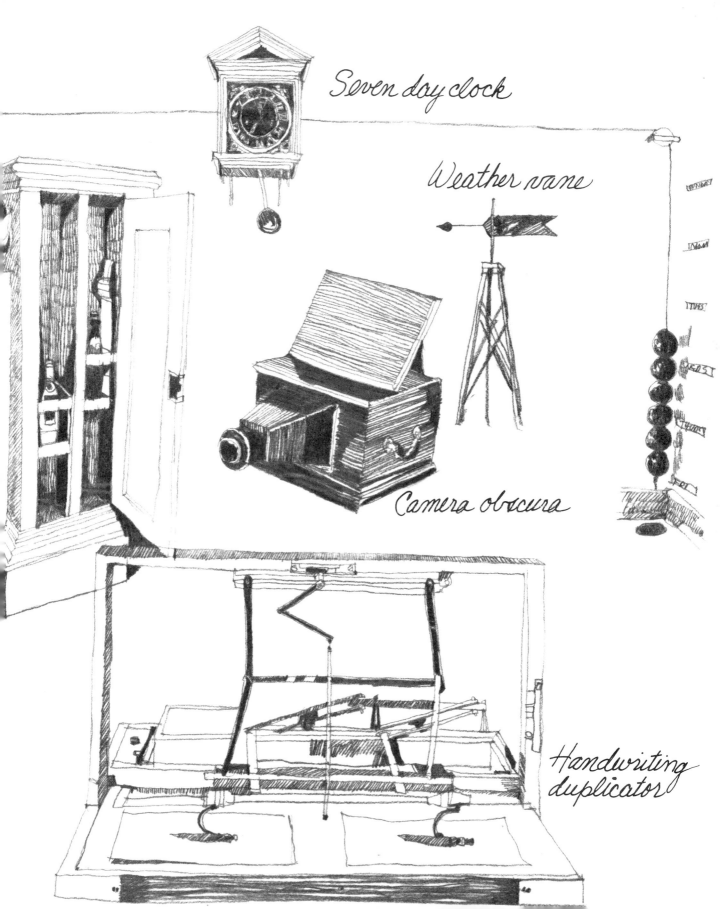

Seven day clock

Weather vane

Camera obscura

Handwriting
duplicator

He was interested in all growing things and approached farming as a science. He improved a mold plow and a threshing machine. He used contour planting on his hillside fields to keep the soil from washing away. He rotated his crops to keep from exhausting the soil.

"I want this house to be a happy one," Thomas Jefferson said. "It should have children in it."

Mr. and Mrs. Jefferson had two little daughters. His sister had eight children, but her husband died of fever and there was no father to care for them.

"Come and live with us," Jefferson told his sister. "There is plenty of room in our big house. I will act as the father for all the children."

Soon Monticello was a happy, lively place. Children laughed and played on the lawn and in the meadows around the house. Jefferson was a kind father to all the youngsters. Parts of the house were still being built, and the children liked to watch the carpenters sawing boards. They watched the masons building new walls with bricks. Sometimes they helped the servants milk the cows and bring the vegetables in from the gardens.

The servants liked Jefferson, too. He was always kind to them, and if they were sick he made sure they were taken care of. The house cost so much to build that sometimes he didn't have any money. But vege-

tables and wheat were grown on the plantation. There were cows for milk and other animals for meat. Everyone always had enough food to eat.

"I love Monticello," he said. "I wish I never had to leave here."

But he was always having to leave his mountain home. He continued to serve in the House of Burgesses for seven years after his marriage, for ten years altogether.

These were eventful years for all the colonies. Even before Jefferson and his bride moved into Honeymoon Cottage, British soldiers in Boston had fired into a crowd and killed three men. This became known as the Boston Massacre.

Tension grew between the colonists and England, but the king did not back down. Three unsettled years went by. Then one cold December day in 1773 some British ships arrived in Boston harbor loaded with tea. The colonists said, "We will not drink this tea if we have to pay taxes when we buy it, and if we can buy it only from the British East India Company and not through our own merchants. Turn your ships around and go back to England." But the ships stayed in the harbor.

One night soon afterward, a group of colonists dressed as Indians climbed aboard the ships, tore open the chests of tea, and dumped them in the harbor. The next morning the water was brown with British tea.

When news of this "Boston Tea Party" reached Virginia, Jefferson knew that it would not be the end of trouble. It was not.

The British closed Boston Harbor thinking that the Massachusetts colony would be cut off, since contact between the colonies at that time was by sea. Virginia and the other colonies sent supplies overland. The American colonies, for the first time, were acting like one united country.

The trouble grew until real fighting broke out. In April of 1775, General Gage sent seven hundred of his British troops marching on Concord where the colonists had stored ammunition. Paul Revere and William Dawes rode out on horseback and warned the farmers and other patriots that the British were coming.

There is now a marker at Lexington with the words of the American Captain Parker on it. He told the patriots, "Stand your ground. Don't fire unless fired upon. But if they mean to have war, let it begin here."

Eight Americans were killed and the Revolutionary War began. The British went on to Concord, but were driven back to Boston. They were not driven out of Boston until George Washington took command of the American forces in the war that dragged on for seven more years.

Soon after the fighting had begun in Boston, Jefferson was sent to Philadelphia to the Continental Congress. The people in each colony had voted to declare the colonies an independent country. Jefferson was chosen to write the Declaration of Independence.

He worked for two weeks writing, rewriting, choosing the right words. When the Declaration was accepted by members of the Continental Congress the colonies became a free and independent country.

King George did not let his American colonies go without a fight. He sent more soldiers and ships to fight this new nation, and the war went on for several years.

Thomas Jefferson, a member of the Virginia House of Burgesses, worked for the defense of Virginia. The capital was moved to Richmond and Jefferson was governor of the state when the war finally ended. Richmond was a little nearer to Monticello and he could get home more often. But he could not stay there for he was still called upon to serve his country. He was sent as a minister to France. Then when Washington was elected President, Jefferson was made his Secretary of State. It was a ten-day trip from New York to Monticello.

John Adams became President and moved into the White House in Washington. Jefferson was the Vice-President under Adams. Then he was President himself for eight years. Washington, however, was much closer to Monticello than New York was.

Jefferson kept his faith in the hard-working poor people, and always fought for government by and for all the people of the country.

At last the time to retire came, and a happy Thomas Jefferson went home to the house he loved. The children had grown up and there were grandchildren. Jefferson was always setting up schedules of study for them. Nature study and French in the morning, dancing classes in the afternoon, reading in the evening. The children had the freedom of the house and grounds, except for one room. That was Mr. Jefferson's study. They always knocked before they entered.

Retirement did not mean idleness for Jefferson. There was the farming to be improved. There were changes to make in the house, although people were saying it was the most beautiful house in America. At one time, he decided the beautiful big stairway took up too much room, so he had it torn out and put in two narrow little secret stairways to the second floor. He designed homes for his friends and gave advice to others who were building. Jefferson's influence on the architecture of many Virginia buildings can be seen today.

His fame as an architect grew and he was asked to design the buildings for the University of Virginia at Charlottesville. Jefferson worked hard at this. Since Charlottesville was just a few miles from Monticello, there were days when he could sit on his mountain and watch the progress of the work on the buildings through a large telescope. Many of his buildings are on the beautiful campus today.

Monticello, high and serene on its mountaintop, was seldom quiet. Its owner longed for the life of a

farmer, free to spend many hours in his study. But he was a wise and famous man who had spent forty years in public service. People flocked to his home to see him. There were friends. There were statesmen from all over the world. Sometimes the house had as many as fifty guests at one time. The gracious house was big enough to hold all of them, but feeding them sometimes became an expensive burden.

When the University of Virginia opened at Charlottesville, Jefferson was asked to come and be its

Monticello

University of
Virginia

State
Capitol

head. He was an old man, but he served gladly because he believed so strongly in the importance of education. The university was close to his beloved Monticello, so he was able to ride to it every day in a carriage and come home at night.

He enjoyed strolling around its grounds with his grandchildren, or reading quietly in his library. "All my wishes end," he once wrote, "where I hope my days will end, at Monticello."

Jefferson died on Independence Day, July 4, 1826, when he was eighty-three years old. His days ended at Monticello as he wished and he was buried on the grounds. The monument over the grave has these words engraved upon it, also as he had wished.

HERE WAS BURIED
THOMAS JEFFERSON
AUTHOR OF THE
DECLARATION
OF
AMERICAN INDEPENDENCE
OF THE
STATUTE OF VIRGINIA
FOR
RELIGIOUS FREEDOM
AND FATHER OF THE
UNIVERSITY OF VIRGINIA

Today Monticello is owned by a patriotic organization called the Thomas Jefferson Memorial Foundation.

The house and the grounds are kept in beautiful condition, just as Jefferson kept them himself. Visitors come from all over the world to see this home that was loved so much by a great American. Even today, people marvel at the design of the house and the inventions of Jefferson that were built into it.

The house called Monticello tells us much about the man who was farmer, architect, statesman, President, inventor, educator—a genius whose mind was never idle. He was a man who built a house with bricks and also helped to build modern America in the days when self-government was an experiment. He is remembered for his faith in the common sense and honesty of the people, and his belief in freedom of the individual, of religion, and of the press.

About the Author: Norman Richards grew up in a small New England town. A descendant of early colonial settlers, he developed a love of history as a child. He holds a journalism degree from Boston University and has traveled over much of the world in his career as a writer and magazine editor. He is the author of fifteen books for young people and more than one hundred magazine articles on aviation and travel. Mr. Richards now lives with his wife and three children in the wooded countryside of Connecticut, not far from New York City.

About the Illustrator: Chuck Mitchell presents a creative new approach to editorial illustration. He has, through his intensive research and unusual artistic approach, avoided all stereotypes. His valid portraits effectively convey the unique atmosphere of each historical period. Intensely evident is the character of each man and woman whose individual acts combined to make history.